AF091605

byzantine

byzantine

theodore michael christou

First Edition

Hidden Brook Press
www.HiddenBrookPress.com
writers@HiddenBrookPress.com

Copyright © 2017 Hidden Brook Press
Copyright © 2017 Theodore Michael Christou

All rights for poems revert to the author. All rights for book, layout and design remain with Hidden Brook Press. No part of this book may be reproduced except by a reviewer who may quote brief passages in a review. The use of any part of this publication reproduced, transmitted in any form or by any means, electronic, mechanical, photocopied, recorded or otherwise stored in a retrieval system without prior written consent of the publisher is an infringement of the copyright law.

byzantine
by Theodore Michael Christou

Cover Photograph – Theodore Michael Christou
Cover Design – Richard M. Grove
Layout and Design – Richard M. Grove

Typeset in Baskerville Old Face
Printed and bound in Canada
Distributed in USA by Ingram,
    in Canada by Hidden Brook Distribution

Library and Archives Canada Cataloguing in Publication

Christou, Theodore Michael, 1978-, author
    Byzantine / Theodore Michael Christou. -- First edition.

Poems.
ISBN 978-1-927725-28-3 (softcover)

    I. Title.

PS8605.H7554B99 2017   C811'.6   C2017-900432-8

for desdemona

for the shepherds of this arid space

θάυτικα.
και ξύπνησα θαμμένος.
βουβός. θολός και πνιγμένος, σε
βάθος σαράντα χρόνια. είχα
αποκοιμηθεί, με ένα θρήνο
αγκαλιά. ήταν αυγή,
και το χιόνι έπεφτε σαν χύμα.
τον βλέπαμε τον χειμώνα. άβολα,
χωρίς έννοια.
σκεφτόμουνα πώς το χιόνι έχωνε τον κήπο
και την μικρή μας την αυλή.

σε ελάχιστο χρόνο
είχα κι εγώ χωθεί. κάτω από
το χιόνι. και πιό κάτω
από το χώμα.

μου είναι
γνωστός ο χειμώνας.

και χάνομαι συνεχώς.

the poet weeps at his window. the windowsill, wet, brick-and-mortar, withstands the weight of the weeping writer's skies.

i envy him as he loathes me.

the moon is coy tonight, episodically beaming despite the darkness and burrowing in the lazy clouds. the sun has never meant to be as marvellous.
the poet weeps at his window.

if his skin he could trespass and shed, his running from his head would now no hesitation cause. if feet were ever forcibly pressed against the ground, if songs were ever subtle, if wishes were to fancies real, then this young poet in his sorrow sobbed.
many have it worse. many have no windowsill at all.

but that poet, between sobs, between breaths, murmurs lyrics of a love song fables taught him long ago.

the poet incessantly skirts from horizon to horizon on the plane of epiphany. skipping stones as a practice of consciousness.

skipping stones along the plane of worlds.

his thoughts are the weeds, where the stones, like seeds, fall, and find asphyxiation.

you would read his thoughts in an instant, in the moistness of his eyes.
yet his thoughts are gone and past before you might hear them.
the context has already changed.

imagine, then, the same space. ages apart. eyes transfixed.

picture him instead at a window, elbows on the sill, head in the clear sky.

he is mute.
imagining lines.

i sat down by the current night and watched it turn to grey or black and white.
a moon slipped by.
and then some light.

the current lulled my friends to sleep,
and on these shoals they curled to dream of silky, and of cushioned, sheets.

i stood to stretch my weary back. to walk amidst the grey and black. to mock the night. to think and tussle.

amidst the black and white and light.

i dreamt one night of forgiveness.
in quotidian time and place.
there was daylight marking its absence. so i entered a cavernous space.

it was lit up like a cathedral.

as a supplicant i stuttered, seeking solace and prayer and rest.

then you took my hand. i knew you.
i could scarcely see your face.

it had been years since i had touched you. but i knew that i was safe.

this is the winter solstice of my mind.
it fades too soon to darkness.
it takes too long to wake.

upon waking, all is ice.

winter hung as a mist in the air in the morning.

fresh-breathed, it exhaled hints of mint and juniper.

it all was shamelessly grey.

in the late afternoon, it held on dearly.

the sun receded.

day darkened, lending a hazy texture to the sky.

that was lazy and sweet.

there was a time of sonnets. a time of byron. i sang to you with capitalized nouns. with rhyme and exclamation.

there was a time of whirring. you seemed to be spinning and i sought to capture your impression in motion.

there was a time of stillness, of scratching and subtle composition in snow-laden red brick.
i leaned and stretched to reach you, pressing my chest against the window trim, reaching for words.

the night makes me remember.
it is the quiet.
anger subsides.
sometimes i pray
and plan what to make of myself once i wash all the crust off my dreaming in subsequent days

it is the stars. the moon. the quiet. the subsumed rage. it is the mirrors in my home, which sometimes reflect a visage that is better and sometimes a body that is more subtle and aged.

it is the softness of time. the respite from the heavy light. the various indulgences that i permit.

i remember the man who ought and the one who should.

mostly, i remember you.
i recall that i almost forgot you. that the shape of your eyes is the greatest indulgence. that i write for you with an increasingly fractured pose.

at night, i look upon you as you are, not as i see you. you are my paradox, more visible in starlight than in phosphorescence.

i put off sleep and waking, the noise, the rage, the pursuant day. i compose volumes of recollection and imagining.

sometimes i plan.
sometimes i pray.

reader, i light the spark of life.
what a gracious gift – not living in a vacuum.
my fire feeds on oxygen as i do. we share this
bond and i seal our love with a kiss.
my mate fills me with darkness, and
i rejoice.
this is love – fire we breathe and consume and crave.
darkness that billows from our sightless loss.
i love, and i weep. underlooking the stars.

i seek you, love,
on a night of blowing trees,
when the back door opens and the volume of the rustling leaves seems
too akin to dreams.

i am on tips and toes.
it is late and it is dark.
the paint peels quickly. the black is stark.

i seek you, love, in every ounce of space. nostalgia leaks.
i waver and creep.

i stood through eons, dark and black, hunched as i remain against this
wall. a cold wind blew.
but it was at our backs.

i remember your dark hair, your black dress, your eyes, your name.
you wore boots.
we took an elevator ride. you were transformed by my meagre cloth.

there was teriyaki, indigo blue, and a something breakfast. we took every mode of transport and applauded fireworks, both mediocre and sublime.

i had time in the hospital, presaging it all before it came, as if it were a playlist that i had heard before.

from here, then, on my window perch,
i replay the memory of another time,
perhaps yesterday night, when i held this
statuary position.

there was a smokestack on the crest of a
house.
in the winter air, the smoke was beautiful.
like breath it danced. this was a furnace breathing, not fire, not
logs.
if the house were a boat and the frosted snow that on
the yard and driveway slept were waves, the smoke might have billowed similarly.

there is a solemn sadness in the loneliness of this vision.

my eyes do not see. there is a
necessary isolation in imagining. the moon, looking at us in the clean but biting icy air must feel like i do, though there is no consolation in this thought.
through an open window.

i am alone again, observing.
were this a song, this snowy isolation would be my chorus.

perhaps it is the absent soundtrack that i am
lamenting. music has a way of being understood,
while words are skimmed over and shattered.

somewhere in my distressed, through-window-peering, self
i hold ambitions of a spirit. this spirit is
insubstantial. it craves flesh.

spirit broods, reflecting.
flesh clicks intemperately at a keyboard.

they are shadow and light, soul and body.

notion and reality.

word and blank page. prisoners unto each other.

the keys tap as if they were looped on the belt of a prison guard. the soul casts the body into a cell, and the opposite is equally true. the words liberate and restrain.
neither believes in the existence of the other.

polyglot are these patchwork testimonials. coded in cacophonous bleats.

these are abhorrent, unbathed.

loving and romantic, even.

there are beautiful notions expressed in awful language. by the stringing together of very ugly sounds

like paintings of black and grey.

i stand as a bound man murmuring and binding, each instant, a self.

my fancies free me.
because a fairy wisdom is an easier deception to imagine.
because i have read of the transcendental.
because i must will myself to be awake
even though i have woken and cursed the foulest damnations upon the sun.

and so i weep. in the hole in the wall,
in the chasm nothing of his window.

the chasm, a wintered silhouette of ink.
it stains parchment with its mocking form.

i hope some twirling sentence to unfurl.

i hope some swirling sentence to uncurl.

and if the moon were cracked,
then the stars her sparkling specks became.

this night, they dance as if the sky was a nightclub pageant.

the motions of the cosmos
spin the spheres in tune with me.
the shapes of dragons shake and shine,
the hunters hound, the hounds pursue the stinging tails, and tales my
conscience turns.

these stories like the star specks glow.
the music-spinning-worlds in honeyed rhythm flow.

since i am torn, my land is too.
my nation is a poet and a peasant.
a shepherd and a lion heart.

i think in desert-ancient tongues and find my freedom in germanic ink.

my land and i are a karst topography.
stone, mountain, sand, my skin. sinkholes, caves, and wells, my soul.

so floods of foreign tongues, with licking
flames, parched skin and sand.
scratched paths askew mountain peaks.
befriended figs and jasmine. the rocks remind of bloodloss and hymns
to hope.

waving waters of the middle sea wash the shells and sand. washing,
they foam, as foretold my hesiod and the mythologians.

desire steps from the sea's embracing chasm step with naked-breasted
newness.

my father made me thus.

when he armed himself and walked the pastures late, and learned to make a bed by scratching the frame of one upon the earth, i sat there short of breath.

i learned that our absence made our families mourn us as if we were already passed.
for many lives had past on in these fields.

we sat like thieves amongst the lambs and the sheep.
we counted stars. like flecks of the divine. or of a sparkling moon
like lit lambs in a dark pasture.

beneath the guardian moon.
loving something lost.

we were shrouded in grace
swaddled as babes
and light

now we twitch in the night
prompted by dreams to forgive ourselves relentlessly
treating ourselves like innocents and children

we twitch
unrestrained in mind and space
unfettered by time
unbound and godless, we quiver in the night

i lost myself some years before. some thousand years before my memories told.
i lost myself, as tales unfold, beneath the moon, when naught was old.

a fig, of the tree of life, i ate. or, of a lemon tree.
or some slice of quince.
i know i've tasted these fruits before.

some, it is said, mounted the queen of england.

they framed her face and mounted the frame upon their walls.

during the inspections, she would look out upon the empire.
she would otherwise have her alabaster skin cast against the plaster of the wall.
whenever elizabeth concentrated on plaster,

whichever way she glared, poets were hung for writing odes.
and clemency was perpetually a few hours delayed at the gallows.

the morning waned as the sounds grew longer and more acute.

the sheets became more burdensome. i rolled onto your vacant pillow.

full of guilt. each minute was a moment of flesh hugging silk that grazed the skin of my fingers. i saw your face in flashes, as lucid dreams. moments past as half hours.

then, i lost you.
it was morning.
i was awake.

the moon gives rise to miscreant things.
i was born, not at midnight, but in moonlight.

i, for where memory fails, the mind prevails.
and i was not born with this country.
she is not
me and i am not her.

you tapped my thigh, interrupting nothing.
you nodded as a gesture so that my sight might pursue the direction of our gaze. i pursued, gazing in tune.
each inch of the dwarfish mount we looked upon was populated. built upon. i imagined each home as a happy space.

flooded by light and heat, i contemplated living otherwise.
life could be.

take me there. to the mount. to july. and i shall be well
and perchance, there, sleep.

no, i am not cyprus.
she does not, save in the
mind of a new generation and
of some acute mapmakers, breathe.
she is not.

she came to me, with parched and ensanguined
lips. i pursued her through narrow concourses
and parochial passes. i bathed myself in her warmth,
here, in the cradle of aphrodite. i bottled fragile filaments of foam, there
where the stony shore accosts the sea and engenders it.
i scabbed, where i found scars left by foreign armies.
i clawed at my eyes
where a crescent moon scratched itself upon olympus. i roared with the
fury and rage of othello and there she hid.
masked in garish pageant, lit by the counterfeit,
ephemeral flash of a camera's light. our eyes met,
and she staggered across the slates and athwart the stairways that collapsed
in the blasts of napalm blasts. i see no
thing but sense my passage through streets upon which my parents trod.
between laborious breaths choked with
heat and ash, i hear the beckoning lyric of the sirens. on this isle they
chant byzantine hymns of a bygone time, forgotten.
i think of passion, and shoulder historically appalling anamneses as i theo-
rize upon fanciful meditations of the elusiveness of life
wrought by ages of my oppressed kin. and as i feel my hamlet surge i
kneel, overcome
by the tickling scent of jasmine. and i am enlaced in the
embrace of my native soil, which time and fate forgot. and
i choke with love. and i am enamoured by the
decaying beauty of this land. pursuing my
madness a pistol glares. so in midstride i see a green line. it is made of
sandbags and grief. of hollow bricks.
of dust, like this land.
i hear the imam call.
the orthodox chant differently and likewise.

i kneel. touch the earth.
kiss the spastic asphalt in a sporadic in a prayer. and from my knees, i
wash myself with ritual weeping, leaving all but art, and sing.

we have known frost, night, and diet.
in the name of love and rage, we bridged continents.

it is a bosporus, this love.
it knows politics, not quiet.

snow falls subtly.

i long for you today, in warmth, and in the clutches of winter.

throughout autumn, in despair,we turn from green to blue.
the spring rain bears no remedy.

let all the seasons rot.

you are the sun. the moon. the acid earth. the icy stars.

thank all ethereal heavens for disquiet. this love is and it is not.

the night gleans from me too much.
it skims my thoughts from the surface.

the moon is monolithic, but not shy.
it makes me look to myself more. and it stares.

turn my eyes inward, susceptible to this overlooking i.

come to me dreaming, nightshine,

turn this inner eye on me, in image self, to see.

come, all are one.
and all these that i know are none,

and all i know is naught but me.

love, you are idea.

we whisper of paradigms, of plato, and of our dreams.

whilst the night hums, assonance serves to calculate the earth and its axis. pre-socratics make levers of us and of the world. it was quiet once, upon the world. today we are all compelled to be philosophical.

icarus has given way to sisyphus. irrevocably, we are in the midst of an existentialist age. we are damned to roll and churn the world even as we whir irrevocably within it. we toil, amidst the rubble and it's various hills, in a time of unrequited rhyme.oh but there is so much to see, to spend, to taste;

alas for our red-dry eyes, alas for the cost, and regrets. alas that we both shall die.

oh, but today i do not hear the fearful rumble of chariot steel.

for hades, too, has much to do.

i woke a son. i embrace greying and bloated form of a man. i drive home,
a drummer boy. night falls,
and i am none.

there are others too, in me. shards with gaps like veins between them.
minute by minute,
i skirt between the ragged edges like an itinerant comedy troop of players.

the dizziness is too slight to spur me to immediate sleep. i turn my gaze inside.
i overlook, and look at dreaming, dreaming life. the moon, reflecting, rears a
spurting chaos of disconsolate disorder in this head.

i overlook from the perch on this windowsill.
the music in the background is lost in the self-absorbing gazing of the cosmos.

i see the night as it might appear from a thousand vantage points or more.
but all i think about is me.

i find my
legs stretching beneath my torso, lifting me gently
from my perch.
i keep stirring, until i stand as
upright as an average amassment of flesh and bone.

i stand, then, at my window.
perched. this day, strung up.

i sense the shadows shifting between the lights of night and day.

a string puppet. strung between dreams and days.

i stand alone because my dreams pervade my days.
afforded neither. nor love,
nor guarantees, nor certitude.

it is difficult to breathe.
the air is all of pollen and spores.

spring pollutes my lungs. beauty brings perils.

my body chokes out my stirring spirit, which can no longer see the moon
or, even, me.

despite myself, i drank my tears again.

there are three creative forces

god is the first. we are the second. the objects we fashion are the third.

this third, along with the second, is an inimitable part of the first. i was enmeshed in a long debate about this position with an excellent philosopher. she seemed to best me, i think, but only in zealotry.

this is no apostolic preaching. this is the meditation of a monastic at the edge of a world.

from here, i cannot see where the sky ends and the aegean opens. the air above and the sea below are woven of the same cadency and blue.

this mountain vantage view and the world i see are the playing out of raw potentiality.

i believe in a prime mover, as aristotle reasoned. all of evolution is inertia. we are creatures that create. so we twitch. and then lie still. still fabric of a creative force

here is a dream that met me near dawn this morning: i step
into a church darker than night. afire
are a thousand candles, thousand
blessings, thousand all-uplifting-wings. i take a
candle too and light it, and i know i am not here alone.
i take her hand, she is a thousand wishing candles and
my own, and, and my own.

there is no peace to mirror this.
there is none that i have known. i understand
what quiet is. i understand now calm.
some sweetness starts inside of me and fuses two
to one. all yesterdays and morrows seem so innocent and young.

i want more light to understand this human form
that holds me here. i turn my eyes from hers
and scan the chasm dark within. between each of the thousand lights there is
such dark as even one's imagining could never but suppose.
some fear my outstretched fingers skims, and it, a
viper's poison bite, in seconds seeks my heart.
i turn to her to hold her round the shoulders, out of fear.
i turn to her and, turning, wake. and waking, weep, alone.

i dreamt the dream of dreams last night.
as byron did dream dreams.
in greek.
in messolonghi.

this until ottoman cannon burning turned to solace.
as shelley did dream to dream.
to revolt.
to tire.

this until the tempest turned to silent peace.
in another middle sea.

we walked slowly like the limestone.
i recall that there was much to say.
i was a pace or two ahead of you.
it was difficult to speak.
and we were distracted by architecture.

our hands brushed.
i slowed my pace.
shortened my gait.
held my words.
yours were beholden to yourself.

i, morose and golden, held my pose.

we woke to gasp for the flesh of each other in a cot too small and slight.

sometimes you caught me, light and wailing. at other times more, i held you tight.

once, we sat on rotting timbers. twice we pioneered a home. thrice we walked around stone ruins. for the fourth time, we eloped. five drear times, the snow kept falling. there were six days on the road. on a seventh day, we rested, and we made a pyre of the codes.

i have stood outside at night to conjure words and constellations. you have frowned and rubbed my back, amidst the bridges and stone roads. we have danced, despite the murmur, casting out our gems and clothes.

we have sat in still and darkness.
days have crawled but years have lapped. we have kept each other warm. through the silence. in the storms.

a white expanse of place and time.
not sweat and blood, but snow.

i dream of cypress trees and rapids. of the
canadian shield. of scarred cliffs.
i conjure crass waterfalls and foamy
stones.

someone else has trotted here. there are
footprints sunken, still.

this lake is only pallet.

though the white of snow is blank, it re-
mains subject to our many eyes, our many
woes, our appetites, our sighs.

i see the purity of ice, though it is cold and
sparse. i see myself, downtrodden, frail, re-
flected in the whites.

these are our renaissance lives.
epicurean and atomistic.

these are serene and quiet gardens. fruits of
this life. labors and pains.

these are our renaissance sighs.
tying us to marble. to the selves that we con-
truct. to innovation and renovation.

we sit upon a stoic steed, as if we were com-
neni, bearded and cast on high.

this is our renaissance. these palpitations are
percussion. god stamps and roars around us,
while we, petty and promethean, keep time.

ouranos, the sky,
gave birth to cronos, time, and to other titans.
these titans held dominion over the world.
time, castrated the sky, taking from him his crown.

the blood poured into the sea, off the coast of my land.
and beauty was born from the foam.
upon the crashing rocks, amidst the salt and noise.

within us is all of mythology.
we are the sky, living in time, contemplating beauty.
we are the scarred, the ones who scar, and the salt, foam, and sea.

here is all of heaven and earth.
of prophesy and pain.
violence and redemption.

it is a sinister time.
and we feel it in the mindless funk of this radio age.

though i do not comprehend elgar or Schubert,
i see an assonance with a world bereft of key and tonal base.

in the rituals to which we acclimatise our ears.

it is a classical time.
we are in the first movement of a machine age.

and i listen with 1913.
tuned to cubism,
and to the rhymes of freud.

these are the early decades of a very young century.
there is pride in being avant guard.

there is a small stravinsky in our dreams.

there is a composition crawling up our spines.

the moonlight implored my sighs to open.
modestly, i looked away.
having sworn never to sing of sighs again.

i swore once more.

the time of moans.
of sighs.
of other sounds replete with -oz- has passed away.

do not mourn
my bones are cleaned.
my rot is lost.
ancient porphyry and two-pronged forks are lodged between my cracks.

i am both seed and soil.

so no not weep.
rest, work, toil, and sleep.
i will see you soon, my love, before the snowfall.
after the harvest of a soon-time harvest is reaped.

my father kept his father's herd at night, and took it to some grazing hills far far away. for cyprus, under foppish rule,
was poor, and destitute and dry.
my mother and some other mothers, tended to each other while their husbands tended sheep. and if an owl called it meant, to some superstitious and worrying minds, that death was near.
such was the context and the myth.
and the ladies mourned and wailed and sang the sorrow-fullest songs.

i left at this and went to find the rolling hills. to escape the mourning.

we scratched the dusty ravaged earth and slept in its embrace.

this earth, she held me many times. her wells are wells of tears, drowning generations of my mothers and sisters.

it is the middle sea, and arid. so the earth depends on its women's tears to stay alive.
water is rationed, but sorrow flows freely.
as food was rationed, as dreams were rationed,
the women of my world were given rationed lives.

i long for mother.
as all seems lost and futile.
as sleepless nights morph to sleepy days.
As unrest escalates.

as i forget those stories that steadied me as a child.
whenever i sensed angst and fear,
which are now both too commonplace.
which harass. which debase.

my mother would hold me with words.
and tell me stories of crafty minded.
or of noble hearted feats.
of courage of hope.

i long for mother.
mother of the craftiest mind.

of brave feats.

when i falter in courage and hope.

it is a tin-roof doldrum, from dusk till dark.
we lie alone. we wake. we twitch.

tall is the spring, and the brown snow melts.

somewhere the sun has begun to disrobe.

somewhere the water foams.
some ice is breaking.

someone is peering and hoping for more.

doubts are receding in our morning minds.

galaxies burn.

the hours click.
i have absolved all of us us for this day.

i scratch a bed upon some sand my shepherd father and his shepherd father bought. i have some dusty sand and rock to lay upon, when i retreat from my window sill, the smokestacks, my weary breathing, and my self. on this dust my father and his father slept.

this earth is scratched and scarred. it has a crescent moon
and star incised upon its face.
the mountains and the plains are made our slaves. marked forever by our violence.

in the distance, the water smacks upon the stones, engendering foam. beauty coexists with horror. spirit and skin still share a space.

i inherit this scratched out bed of earth.
i curl inside a scratch i've made for me.

a me-shaped form asleep i see.
i've inherited some land.
some starvation.
and some scars.

the greek word for carved
also signifies a proclamation that day has dawned.
the light carves through the day.

crawling from my scratched space on the earth,
i am likewise carved.
sliced by a crescent sun.

we were lovers of wisdom
and demonstrated our affection for words
by lying on the grass and crafting
images out of silhouette clouds.

it was a bright day.
and the grass was trim.
and the lunch we ate digested.
and we were younger than we are presently.

walkers walked.
we lay, belly up upon the grass,
which we later rubbed off each others' backs.

we were poor.

i woke with the sun, which carved out the sections of the day.

mother awoke before the sun.
she had fried potatoes for our breakfast.

these were red and salty. hard and hearty. like the earth.

i would take off my
white collared shirt and my blue
pressed pants with love, gently.
i pressed my pants and washed my own white shirt by hand in a
basin with handsoap.

once, i tore my shirt on a thorn bush walking in the schoolyard.
if i wore this shirt to school the next day everyone would know that it was
my only one.
i stitched small stitches, sobbing.
no one noticed.

each was too preoccupied with the concealment of their own stitches.

we would thresh the fields once a year. gather wheat.
carry it to the mill. pay the miller with
our labour's fruits. with what we
sold, we would pay the loans. the school. the milk man. mend our walls.

we could not sit idly by the windowsill.
seeing the moon and stars and thinking upon ourselves.

we could not afford poetry.

this is no time to be ornate.

it is beautiful to look upon you, mother.
your beauty needs neither flowers, nor blush.
you sit in a bathrobe working upon a crossword. your
glasses look crooked, and they sit awkwardly athwart
your face. your hair is disheveled, as it always seems to
be when you are worried. each time that i must travel,
you imagine the worst.
those large eyes of yours dart.

you have been awake since dawn, it seems like, cooking.
i am visiting for the day, and you've made that day a
feast. it is thanksgiving each day that i visit. i have thanks
to give for these moments, albeit brief.

it is beautiful.
and the simplicity of this beauty will later lull me to
sleep.

i walked for days in the pages of poets lost in the foliage.

i have worked for many days here in the forest of our words.

i smell of sage and pine needles.

on the first night here, i scratched myself and bled.
on the second, i sat amidst the quiet and read.
for five whole days i found some quiet in a scratched-out bed.

and then the pollen struck me. and i rested.

down by the wet stones where our bones began to break, the horizon was washed out by minuscule waves that reflected the sun.

under the winking eye of a crescent moon, wrought iron and turquoise clay paved a pathway, which we effortlessly trespassed.

we may have lain on grass, which seems improbable, and read the bits of byron and keats that seemed romantic.

the sun set one year ago to this day, then we sought a place to play near a memory laced with doubt.

we walked between books. pet a cat. dined. doubted all our dreams. doubled down. frowned. and woke to grasp beside the bed for the flesh of each other. five times you caught me groaning.

once, we sat on rotting timbers. twice we pioneered a home. thrice we walked around the ruins. for the fourth time, we eloped. five lone times, the snow kept falling. there were six days on the road. on this seventh day, we rest, and we set fire to the codes.

i have stood outside your thoughts at night, conjuring words and constellations. you have frowned and rubbed my back, in a frail feline imitation. we have danced, despite our wishes. we have toiled betwixt the storms.

days have crawled.
six years have sprinted.
we have kept each other warm.

once upon a time, maybe even today:

i kicked a can. it was exuberant ecstasy.
in a parking lot,
i kicked a pop can.
it was full, but i did not know that it was full as it had been opened.
my foot hit it squarely in the centre.
a cylinder does not actually have a centre,
i know. this can, struck at the
midpoint of its height, lifted and flew.

my leg, bent slightly at the knee,
sent the can up upright and farther, far farther,
than i had imagined probable. i did not measure how far exactly.

it is rare than life exceeds expectations.

this was not a dream.

the can was heavier than empty.
i knew immediately. this only makes my strike more memorable.
picture a can soaring through a parking lot,
not coming down until much later than you expect it to.

it was a moment.

philosophically, it distilled the descartian duality in my mind.
ghost and machine, spirit and body, in civil war.
my body reigned. my spirit, broken, rejoiced.

that was simply a delusion of my hungry head.

in the quiet of the dark, i saw the moon.
it was all crescendo and symbol.

i had a passageway to ancient rome via the too bright constellations in the sky.

i have mocked the light, cowered in caves, and cooled a tepid heart. tonight i am felled by the bitter cold and by cassiopeia.

i long to be held without caveat.

life can be hard and soft. but it is overwrought by halogen and by fluorescent light.

love me beneath the moonlight. in the shade of stars. by the churning chaos of elemental slights.

despite my faults. in spite of strife.

i am sand.
i've been inherited.
i am sea. i crash upon my sand, another elemental form of myself, and foam.

they say that some goddess was born from me, or from some castration.

i am an idea. a concept of beauty, aesthetic.
i am a mother to sand and sea and ideas. to children and to play. to lyric and to art. to war. to too much war.

i cannot speak to your history. i shall leave
that obligation to the victors. it will differ depending on which
flag. which god. which words. you salute.

it will depend on your construction of dualisms.

there was a castrated god. one armed with
lightning and a phallus. one with commandments. one
with love with sacrifice. one with a prophet
and laws.

all is still.

and we are still here writing beneath the wind.
words flow fast like memories and frail images or imaginings.

we slow worlds down, where we can, and cease their spinning or their flight.

whenever we remember to breathe.

i believe in evolution of ideas. in the earth, me. i
evolved into copper.

the land became shards and fragments.
our tears became rivers that course along the shards beneath the dust.

isolation turned to lamentation.

mountains
rose to the sky and crumbled into the sea.

i have an adolescent shade. my sight's a razor in a pallet. in the shade and in between.

but you are red and green and blue. and light and soft.

i stood alone in the light near a pond that was artifice. it was the end of a universe.
the end of life.

beyond, it was all blue. sky, sea, stars. and me.
ether, air, wind.

i thought of metaphysics. of aristotle. of the particles and of the dreams that constitute us.

i am sinew. and stone. and weakness. and bone.

the rest, pond, particle matter, and blue, is inexplicable and fair.

today, i felt the worlds of dreams and dreaming-not were intermingling
in the humid air:

in driving, i took a turn upon a road whose name i knew. it went, as far
as looking told, the same direction as
necessity took me. though i knew it going east,
some five-six minutes north of the oft-passed paths i recognised by
experience, the city from my car lights fled. the schools,
the coffee shops, the building slipped away,
as if they were backdrops on the stage of a viennese opera, set upon a
wheel that would spin and change at the whim of a director.

a graveyard, gated, ancient, took too many seconds for to pass and
frightened me.
like mirrors were the tombstones.

and, to the right, a forest sprung beyond
the rows and rows and rows of sprouting seeds.

the forest, first a marvel in the periphery of
my sight appeared as hydro fields.
like little eiffel towers, all connected.
a hundred twins with electrical umbilical cords feeding each and all.
metal trees, all frankensteins, all keeping guard.

iron masses, animated in my mind.

i am too minute, and i am wasting time.
the intervals are incomplete.
i irregularly think of you;
i think of you.
and i think of you.

there is constancy within the relative.
it breeds regularity.

there is constancy to the irregularity.
and i think of you.

and i think of beauty.

this night is an hour clock.
is a vacuum.
is an atmosphere.
a view/perspective of the moon.

this night is an hour clock.
this is a microbe.
let us endeavour to define its dna.

and i think of you:

vacuum.
atmosphere.
perspective on the moon.

philosophy v beating heart.

this night has a fingerprint.
it is black, and blue, and green.

and i think of you.
a helix: finely spun.

my dna.
a pun

but then. i have seen no colour.

i am alone and the quiet is deep.
the dark is bleak, but not so steep as mythology. there are murmurs in my back. there are shimmers in my mind that twitch and start.

the night open eyed and alert.

winter will come. leaves dangle from the trees. the afternoon is red and yellow and possibly serene.

i cannot see the stars for the clouds. my sighs carry currency in the crisp wind.

long will be my tomorrow.
today has already been.
retreat to bed, i reckon. be soft, unseen.

i have stood in grey light and before dusk
with knuckles worn down by ink and lead
my shoulder blades touching upon our wall
knees clenched
neck taught
stomach protruding
writing words into the air
conjuring as a soft witch might in a withered state.

i have been pagan in an orthodox rite
incanting sounds as soft as sinew
in a world of limestone
to win or woo.

there is a frail white reconnaissance
of ethereal light
drifting around us on this heavy night.

the winter is weaving terrible magic.

walk with me on light and epic.
hold me. i am slight. myopic.
i can not bewitch or pray.

the snow falls bright.
and faith is bold.
i cling to you
with all my might.

and the poet, leaning outside his window,
bent his back to force his shoulders, neck and head outside the frame.

it was the thunder that he heard.

two miles away. lightning then snap. clap clap. clapclap.

the rainfall was cathartic.

the clouds once seemed so far away, just as
dreams form of an artist's sky. round and around. beneath the sun.
beneath the moon. mingled with the specks and stars.

i recall flying home as a child. breaking the plane of the clouds. rising
quickly. expecting to see angels lounging upon the pillows playing
harps unto the lord.

this was not heaven.

i think i called myself naïve.

i served as a monastic for a day.

my face was red and my flesh burned. meters turned to miles, and my uninitiated mind turned to strangers for assurance.

yellow butterflies accompanied my every step.

this foliage sits upon me like a mantle, like a
furry coat. i cling to it absurdly. cannot let
slip off my shoulders.
drawing it around my back and to my heart.
a shawl in which some woman shivers once the sun has slipped
underground to sleep.

i feel the distance between this world and the one that is buried
below has never been so slight. the slumbering sun shines on me
regardless of the dirt between us.

somewhere here, i must scratch a place to sleep.

someone once told me something that was rather silly[1]. i came to think of the comment as less silly only by understanding it's richly personal and associative pleasures.

---

1. onomatopoeia,[2] of a different nature. Όνομα και πράγμα, as we say in greek. name and thing (are of the same essence, hence the same).
2. word associations have great power. silly, as an example, ferries me to the carpet-time circles of kindergarten and to the selectively filtered lexicons of primary teachers whose influence[3] upon the formative years of my existence can only be understated.
3. thank goodness for the formidable corrective energies of what we call human resiliency. potty humour[4] is an invaluable skill. without it, we would lose ourselves in misery.
4. we lean heavily upon these associative meanings of words[5] in order to derive any semblance of pleasure form them. alternatively, we can make up ourwords, ordering them any which way we please. moreover, in so making, we make-up ourselves as poets.
5. though, surely, it must be said, we make up words from words we know. we may only re-create using the recognisable phonemes as lego pieces of our reformation. fifty-six or fifty-eight phonemes are all we have at our disposal. syllables innumerable, although most made-up words that give me any pleasure have only two syllables.[6]
6. there are more colours of crayons in those 64-packs of crayola crayons than there are sounds in the english language.[7]
7. at what point in life, exactly, do we discard our crayon boxes, never to use them again? we graduate to pencil crayon and then to marker and to pastel. these last three tools, along with paints and chalk, are interchangeable and manageable throughout life.[8]
8. just the other day, i noticed a boy playing with a toy that i had as a child, and i had to restrain myself form tackling the little darling of a boy and scurrying to a private corner behind some couch to play. this is how we take words and give them our own meanings.[9]
9. the words we use, make,[10] and remake, and the objects and ideas we represent through these words are keenly personal and subjectively understood. we use words we know.
10. when we make words, we make them of sounds and syllables familiar to us.[11]
11. then, while i am not yet fit to comment on whether or not locke was all right in reference to tabula rasa.[12]
12. as surely as i allude to john locke, he leaned on others for associative meaning.

on a pleasant autumnal afternoon, a beauty once told me that that trees
reminded her of neurons.

her boots made this clip clop on the sidewalk. her stepping made me
hum to myself, adding rhythm to the percussion upon the ground.

startled, i leafed through the pages of an
old psychology textbook that i had imprinted in
my mind. finding a pictured neuron, labeled in the caption neuron, i
superimposed that image on the tree that
reached its twiggy, leafless
branches all around it
just a dozen paces up ahead.

trees were akin to neurons.
or fractals.

in the midst of it all.
the sorrow, the wandering, the fear, and the doubt.

i see the moon.
it is too bright. it is a navel in the sky.

it is dust compacted, whereas i am ghost and all aflame.

there is a reflective rock above us. it shines as a beacon in the darkest hours and our darkest days.

in contrast, i do not shine at all.

i stand on the mezzanine of my mind.
there is a staircase of shadow and light. it is climbing in the
dancing orbit of a dust cloud.

i penetrate too deeply into the whirlwind in
reflection.

there is one self that i imagine and a dozen more to see

i think of each self in its own manner.
it manifests itself as it wishes to be.

green is the colour of nature and of natural ideas. there is a green
line that bleeds in cyprus. it is most unnatural.
green is money and greed.

it is not a primary colour.

i walked this green line for days.
hearing life over the sandbags. through the bullet holes. over the ramparts
and underneath the dancing flag of red and white.

i see copper, white, blue. and red.

these are tugging on the reigns of ire and soot.

in 1960, i imagined union.
of a greater blue and white.

yet this union was purification. it was colourless.

this was no utopia. no melting pot either. nor a dystopian cauldron of bubbling unrest.

but the world was newly postcolonial. we were tired of turning the queen's eyes toward the plaster.

we were ancient, and the curfews seemed as impetuous as an adolescent youth.

as history is arduous, this is a partial story.

of greek princes and the fall of illium. of millenia.
bronze. egypt. persia. rome. byzantium. venetians. ottomans. lion hearts.
lusignians.
red and blue.
gold and black.
solon and othello, and circles that should not be disturbed.

karst. and through the shards and cracks, rivers of tears.
scratches made by many shepherds upon the sand.

we were lucky not to be arrested.

sometimes, the hangman
under- or over-estimates the length of the rope from which one will hang.
and many were hung for less.
for handing out flyers. for writing about freedom. for publishing pamphlets. for requesting union with their heritage.
for living. since only those in pursuit of freedom are alive.

mothers sent telegraphs to london. plead for clemency. visited the embassy, prostrate. weeping. appealing.

sometimes, a death is quick. if the calculations are accurate. your head can be torn from your body if matters are miscalculated. you can hang and die over an arduous eternity as well.

die with the hymn to liberty in your heart.

remember that poets, hanging on their windows, often think of words that move.
captured within themselves, they think to move. to reject the subjugation of skin over spirit.

clemency may come from london.
but it will always arrive a few minutes too late for you to live.

in the meanwhile, divide and
conquer. bomb a building and blame a side. kill a human, condemn another. manufacture consent. construct power.
maintain a presence. write notes of discord, sing them off key, and hold your ears in wonder at the screeching.

take a teacup. point your pinky to the heavens. sip. lament colonial violence.

pax britannica, my shepherd ass.

we repose on these small spheres, which hurtle and churn.

therefore inexorably cast against the elements, twitching and curling. each of us is particle physics, both modern and antique.

i stood aloft. i watched the moon masked by thick clouds. and i knew that i was cast and dyed.

between all the mathematics, i had forgotten that i am soft and small.

i have lost too many words in the well of emotion.

maybe this is not how it happened at all.
something like this did happen, however.

my two earths met, on a dusty road,
framed somehow by my father and by a maple leaf.

the blue berets have gone.
the green line persists.

the star and crescent roar above.
are voracious in the mountain.

the waves of blue may likewise menace other shepherds that i have known
on another side of history.

rusted coils of barbed wire
incongruously contest the copper earth.

till now.
at the earth's closing.
at the foaming of the sea,
and the tempests' breaking

i have spoken in terms endless and bleak.
of the breaking of the earth and of the cracking of me.

i am not other.
i cannot but hope to be.

so i watch from my window.

that there is hope.
that hope is free.

the island was dust. the summers were particularly arid. the sun wrinkled our eyes. its heat baked our lungs, which were full of sand.
we rode out on a tractor to tend to the flock. there was a wooden board that i sat on, looking at history.

we would sit out in the sun baking. from a satchel, he would draw out a large loaf baked in the clay domed woodstove that i would made a mark on each morning as i passed it in the yard. he would carve a perfect slice with the sharpest of knives. then another.

green olives.
hard cheese.

i had been milking goats here over the summer. this was last year's cheese and olives. the brine was distinct.

we sat baking in the sun.
in a land baked by millennia. dry, despite the tears.

amidst the dust. beneath the sun, we feasted.
we ate the fruits of this island place and became part of the earth.
dust and sand.

so, you found your way into my
dreams last night. i don't read
anything into such things. but i figure i
should check ~~up~~ on you

twist the words into a song and you have
poetry, the only thing
of
beauty.

that is exactly what i did. i twisted the words
into poetry. because the words belong to too
many.

and the words are byzantine.

this is my byzantine mind.

turbaned, and foreign unto me.
wrapped in silk and dyed in porphyry.
walled. at once lost to history and emblazoned with gold.

it is dry. and it is caked with the red and the yellow of the earth.
it is all brine, and desiccate.

this is my byzantine mind, mechanical and monastic.
scrawled upon and sinewy. too soft. and hard.

i have watched the fat grow.
curled into grey space.
numbed and been numb.

fallen into the saffron.

Theodore Michael Christou is an Associate Professor of Social Studies and History Education, with a cross-appointment to the Department of History in Queen's University's Faculty of Arts and Science. He began his professional teaching career as an elementary school teacher in Scarborough with the Toronto District School Board. Following a circuitous path, Theodore returned to the academy to pursue doctoral studies in history of education. Dr. Christou commenced his academic course on the tenure track in  Fredericton at the University of New Brunswick in 2009. In July 2012, that course led westwards, back to Kingston, Ontario, and to Queen's University.

Dr. Christou's teaching at Queen's extends to several disciplines; in particular, he concentrates upon history of education, philosophy of education, social studies, and the theory and practice of history.

His research, which spans several fields - history, philosophy, curriculum, and teacher education - is tied together by two questions: a) What is an education for?, and b) How might we imagine an education individual? These questions are bound by historical, as well as contemporary, context and complexities.

Theodore has written academic articles and books, school textbooks, and he has edited numerous scholarly collections and refereed journals. To breathe, he writes poetry, probing self in relation to the other and personal history, mundane and meandering.

www.ingramcontent.com/pod-product-compliance
Lightning Source LLC
LaVergne TN
LVHW040101080526
838202LV00045B/3729